Reading Essentials®
in Social Studies

COUNTRY CONNECTIONS II

BRAZIL

JOANNE MATTERN

Perfection Learning®

Editorial Director: Susan C. Thies

Editor: Mary L. Bush

Design Director: Randy Messer

Cover Design: Michael A. Aspengren

Inside Design: Michelle J. Glass, Mark Hagenberg

IMAGE CREDITS:

© CORBIS: pp. 5 (bottom), 14 (center, bottom), 17 (bottom), 38; AskMaps.com: p. 30; Panelinha.com: p. 33; Getty Images: p. 39; Library of Congress: pp. 21 (bottom), 22

Clipart.com: pp. 5 (top), 7, 8 (top), 9, 10, 11, 14 (top), 18, 19, 24, 25 (bottom), 26 (bottom), 27, 28, 29, 31, 36, 41; Corel: cover, back cover, pp. 34, 35; Map Resources: p. 4; Photos.com: pp. 2–3, 6, 12, 13, 15, 16, 17 (top), 21 (top), 25 (top), 26 (top), 32, 37, 40, 42, 43, 47; Perfection Learning Corporation: p. 8 (bottom)

1 2 3 4 5 PP 08 07 06 05 04
#39615 ISBN 0-7891-6229-6

TABLE OF CONTENTS

Just the Facts! 4

CHAPTER 1 Beneath Your Feet—Brazil's Land and Climate 7

CHAPTER 2 Living Wonders—The Plants and Animals of Brazil 11

CHAPTER 3 Looking Back—Brazil's History 18

CHAPTER 4 Digging In to Brazil's Resources and Industries 24

CHAPTER 5 The Many Faces of Brazil—Discovering Brazil's People . . . 27

CHAPTER 6 A Slice of Life—Brazilian Culture . . . 32

CHAPTER 7 What's Ahead? A Look at Brazil's Future . 41

Internet Connections and
Related Reading for Brazil 44

Glossary 46

Index 48

Just the FACTS!

Location Brazil covers the eastern half of South America. It borders all of the countries on the continent except Chile and Ecuador. The Atlantic Ocean borders Brazil on the east.

Area 3,286,478 square miles

Geographical Features Most of northern Brazil lies within the Amazon **Basin**, which is covered by tropical rain forests. The Amazon River crosses the middle of the region from west to east, where it empties into the Atlantic Ocean. Northeastern Brazil is dry and harsh. The central and southern parts of Brazil contain mountains, **plateaus**, and grasslands.

Highest Elevation Pico da Neblina (9888 feet above sea level)

Lowest Elevation Atlantic Ocean (sea level)

Climate Most of Brazil has a tropical climate. The weather is warm and humid year-round. The southern part of Brazil has a **temperate** climate with cooler temperatures in the winter.

Capital City Brasília

Largest Cities São Paulo, Rio de Janeiro, Salvador, Belo Horizonte, Brasília, Recife

Population 182,000,000 (2003)

Official Language Portuguese

Main Religion Roman Catholic

Government Brazil is a **federal republic**. It is governed by a president. The country is divided into 26 states and 1 federal district.

Rio de Janeiro

WHAT DO WASHINGTON, D.C., AND BRASÍLIA HAVE IN COMMON?

A federal district is an area in a country set aside for the central government. In the United States, Washington, D.C., is a federal district. The federal district in Brazil is Brasília.

5

Industries aircraft, automobiles, machinery, textiles, footwear, chemical products, logging, mining

Natural Resources bauxite, diamonds, gold, iron ore, lumber, rubber, cattle, soybeans, sugar, wheat, rice, coffee, cocoa, citrus fruits

Currency basic unit is the real (RAY ahl)

CHAPTER 1

Beneath Your Feet

Brazil's Land and Climate

Amazon River

At 3,286,478 square miles, Brazil is the largest country in South America and the fifth-largest country in the world. The majority of Brazil's land is rain forest with a tropical climate. Smaller, outlying areas have different landscapes and climates.

> ### THE HIGH FIVE
>
> The five largest countries in the world are Russia, Canada, the United States, China, and Brazil.

GEOGRAPHICAL FEATURES

The Amazon The Amazon extends across almost half of Brazil. The Amazon Basin is the land surrounding the Amazon River and its **tributaries**. The world's largest tropical rain forest—the Amazon Rain Forest—stretches across the basin.

The Amazon River is the second-longest river in the world. It is about 4000 feet long. The Amazon is 1 to 3 miles wide in most places but can be up to 6 feet wide in some spots.

The Amazon begins as a tiny stream more than 17,000 feet up in the Andes Mountains. Hundreds of tributaries join the Amazon along its path. Because of the number of tributaries and the steady rainfall in the region, the Amazon is the largest river in the world. It holds more water than any other river on the planet.

Like all tropical rain forests, the Amazon has four layers. The dark forest floor is carpeted with dead material, such as fallen fruits, leaves, and branches. Above the forest floor is the understory. **Shrubs**, plants, and small trees flourish in this layer. The trees and plants in the canopy grow tall and strong in the sunlight. Some trees reach such great heights that they rise above, or emerge, from the canopy to form the emergent layer.

Emergent

Canopy

Understory

Forest floor

Beyond the Amazon On the far western edge of Brazil is a huge area of wetlands known as the Pantanal. The Pantanal stretches into Bolivia and Paraguay as well. The warm, wet land is a perfect home for many interesting creatures, such as alligators, jaguars, anacondas, and a variety of tropical birds.

A WET WORD

Pantanal means "swamp" in Portuguese.

A large portion of northeastern Brazil is very different from the steamy Amazon. This part of the country is rocky and dry. Sometimes it doesn't rain for years! This harsh land is called the *sertão*.

The northeastern coastal plains lie next to the Atlantic Ocean. Large stretches of **fertile** soil are used for farming. Several big cities are also located in this coastal region.

The central part of Brazil has an area of high mountains that level off into plateaus. The Great Escarpment is a steep slope that drops to a narrow plain along the Atlantic coast. The land here is very rich. Farms, ranches, and mines provide a variety of resources for the people of Brazil.

Southern Brazil has grasslands called *pampas*. The pampas have fertile soil used for farming. The grasses supply grazing cattle with a steady diet.

FALLING FOR BRAZIL

A semicircle of 275 waterfalls crash into the Iguacu River in southern Brazil along the border of Argentina. The Iguacu Falls are more than 2 miles wide and 200 feet high. The most dramatic waterfall is the Garganta do Diablo (Devil's Throat) on the border between the two countries.

THE CLIMATE

Most of Brazil has a tropical climate. The weather is hot, wet, and humid all year long. The average temperature in the Amazon Basin is between 77°F and 86°F the entire year. Rain falls constantly. The western side of the rain forest receives up to 160 inches of rain each year, while the eastern side averages 40 to 60 inches a year.

The northeastern sertão is dry and hot. Temperatures range from 73°F to 91°F. This area receives most of its rain in March and April. Little or no rain falls during the rest of the year.

Along the northeastern coast, the weather is much milder. Steady rain and temperatures in the 80s make this a pleasant part of the country for residents and tourists.

The far southern part of Brazil has a temperate climate. The average temperatures are 50°F in the winter and 82°F in the summer. Frost and an occasional light snow can occur in the colder temperatures.

SHORTS IN DECEMBER?

Most of Brazil doesn't experience seasonal changes. Winter in the rain forest is the same as summer. In southern Brazil, however, seasons do bring slight changes. But these changes happen at different times of the year than they do in the United States. In southern Brazil, the warm summer temperatures occur from December to March. The cool winter months are June to September.

Tourists enjoy the view of Rio de Janeiro from Corcovado Mountain.

CHAPTER 2

Living Wonders

The Plants and Animals of Brazil

The warm, wet climate found in most of Brazil supports an enormous variety of living things. Plants and animals thrive in the country's tropical environment.

PLANTS

Thousands of plants grow in the Amazon Rain Forest. Palm, teak, cypress, and mangrove trees stretch out across the forest. Hardwood trees, such as rosewood and mahogany, stand tall and strong. Huge kapok trees are home to many animals. Other rain forest trees provide foods, such as coffee, cocoa, fruits, nuts, and spices.

Palm

Cypress

Kapok

Bromeliad

Orchid

One of the most common species of rain forest plants are called *epiphytes*. Epiphytes are also known as "air plants" because their roots take in moisture from the air instead of the ground. They also absorb water and minerals from the rain that falls on their leaves. Orchids are epiphytes that produce large, colorful flowers. Bromeliads are short-stemmed epiphytes with tough, curved leaves that collect water.

Climbing plants find a perfect home in the layers of the rain forest. These plants are able to wind and stretch their way up through the bottom layers to reach sunlight in the canopy. Lianas and strangler fig trees are climbing plants found in the Amazon.

GROWING A CURE

At least one-fourth of all medicines used today come from rain forest plants.

SURVIVING THE SERTÃO

The dry conditions found in the sertão make it difficult for most plants to grow. A few cactuses and shrubs that can survive long periods of drought are able to endure the tough land and climate of the sertão.

THE OBVIOUS ANSWER

What is the most common plant in the grasslands, or pampas, of southern Brazil? Grass, of course. Shrubs, bushes, and some small trees also grow on the pampas.

ANIMALS

The Amazon Basin is home to hundreds of mammal species. Many members of the cat family, monkey family, and other groups of mammals roam the forest floor or travel from tree to tree. A larger variety of birds perch in Brazil than in any other country in the world. About 3000 species of fish swim in the waters. A large number of reptiles and insects creep and crawl across the Amazon. Take a look at a few of these interesting creatures.

Jaguar The jaguar is the largest **predator** in South America. It is a carnivore, or meat eater. A jaguar will eat alligators, tapirs, monkeys, deer, frogs, fish, and any other animals it can find. Jaguars can be as long as 8 feet and weigh as much as 300 pounds. These big cats are nocturnal, which means they hunt at night and sleep during the day. They often drop out of trees to attack their **prey**.

Each jaguar has its own territory, or place where it lives and hunts. Because a jaguar often has to travel long distances to find food, its territory can be up to 200 square miles.

Tapir The tapir uses its long nose to pull leaves off bushes that grow on the forest floor. These large animals usually eat at night and spend the day resting in a cool, shady spot. Tapirs also spend a lot of time in the water.

A tapir's body is covered with short, stiff hairs. Young tapirs have striped and spotted coats. These patterns help the animals hide from predators.

Three-toed sloth

Capybara

Vampire bat

Three-Toed Sloth The sloth is the slowest mammal in the world. It spends almost all its life in the same tree, hanging upside-down by its long, sharp toenails. Sloths hardly ever climb down to the ground. Instead, they spend about 18 hours a day sleeping in the tree. When they aren't sleeping, they're eating leaves.

A sloth moves so slowly that a tiny **organism** called *algae* grows on its fur. This algae gives the sloth a green color. Being green helps the sloth hide in the leaves of its forest home.

Capybara The capybara is the world's largest **rodent**. It can weigh up to 200 pounds and measure more than 4 feet long. Capybaras are at home both in the water and on land. The capybara's webbed feet make it a great swimmer. This animal is an herbivore that eats grass and other plants.

Vampire Bat The vampire bat got its name because it feeds on blood. It uses its sharp front teeth to bite the feet and ears of cattle or pigs while they're sleeping. Then the bat licks up the blood.

Like other bats, the vampire bat can soar through the air. It can also jump and run across the ground on its long legs.

Amazon River Dolphin Most dolphins live in the ocean. But Amazon River dolphins can't survive in the ocean's salt water. They live in the freshwater of the Amazon instead. These dolphins are pinker than their sea-living relatives. They feed on many different types of fish.

Toucan Toucans are colorful birds that live in the rain forest canopy. These birds eat fruit and seeds from the trees. Their long bill helps them grab fruits and berries that other animals can't reach.

The toucan's bill is lighter than it looks. The bone underneath the hard shell of the bird's bill is filled with holes. This makes the bill strong but light.

Toucan

Parrot Large flocks of parrots fly high in the canopy. These birds are good fliers and climbers. They use their feet and curved beaks to help them climb. A parrot's strong beak also helps it crack open nuts and slice up fruit.

Parrots are very noisy birds. They use squawks and shrieks to "talk" to one another.

Macaw Macaws are members of the parrot family. They are the largest flying parrots in the world. They are also the fastest.

Like other parrots, macaws have very strong beaks. They use their beaks to break open Brazil nuts. They also have special feet. The two outer toes point forward, and the two middle toes point backward. This helps the macaw climb and carry things.

Macaw

Piranha More than ten species of piranhas swim in the Amazon. Piranhas are usually small and don't appear very dangerous at first glance. But one look in this fish's mouth will frighten you! The piranha's mouth is full of razor-sharp teeth. These teeth, along with the fish's powerful jaws, are strong enough to bite through steel wire. Piranhas are the fiercest freshwater fish in the world. They will attack anything—even people.

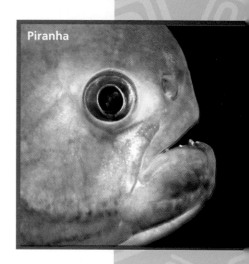
Piranha

Green iguana

Poison dart frog

Green Iguana The green iguana is one of the largest lizards in the world. It can grow up to 6½ feet long. Iguanas are herbivores that eat fruit, flowers, and leaves.

Green iguanas often sun themselves on tree branches to keep warm. But if danger approaches, the iguana can leap away very quickly. Sometimes these lizards bite enemies. They can also use their long, heavy tails as weapons.

Poison Dart Frog The bright colors on a poison dart frog's body warn predators to stay away. Those that don't heed the warning face the frog's unique protective skin. This skin releases poisonous venom. These frogs are so deadly that just touching one can make a person sick.

Poison dart frogs live on the forest floor. When it's time to lay their eggs, these frogs climb up to the canopy. There, they lay their eggs in small pools of water on leaves. Young frogs, or tadpoles, live in these tiny pools until their bodies change into frogs.

Poison dart frogs in other parts of the world need to live in ponds or lakes to stay wet. But the air in the rain forest is so damp that frogs there can live in the trees or on the ground.

Leaf-Cutting Ant More ants live in the Amazon Rain Forest than all other species of animals in the rain forest put together. The most common of these ants is the leaf-cutting ant. These tiny insects live in giant nests below the forest floor. Worker ants spend their days cutting off tiny pieces of leaves. They carry the leaves back to the nest. A **fungus** that grows on the leaves provides food for the ants.

PAMPAS PALS

Two unique animals roam the pampas of southern Brazil. Pampas cats look like large house cats with manes of long hair at the back of their necks. These cats do most of their hunting at night. They eat mice, birds, lizards, and insects.

Pampas deer graze in the grasslands. These small reddish brown deer are endangered because they have to compete with cattle for food.

Pampas cat

CHAPTER 3

Looking Back
Brazil's History

THE FIRST INHABITANTS

The first people who lived in Brazil were Indians. Scientists believe these Indians originally came from Asia about 10,000 years ago.

These early natives were hunter-gatherers. Instead of living in one place, they traveled around looking for food. They hunted for meat and gathered wild grapes, nuts, and other foods to eat.

The Bororo Indians of Brazil hunted, fished, and grew crops in the grasslands of the Mato Grosso region. The remaining tribe members still live in the area today.

Later these Indians settled down and began growing crops and raising cattle for food. By 1500 B.C., the Indians were growing corn. They also grew manioc, which is a root vegetable that can be ground into flour and used to make bread.

Many Indian communities settled along the banks of the Amazon and its tributaries. These communities caught fish from the rivers and hunted animals in the forests along the banks. They were also able to farm on the fertile land.

Some ancient Indian tribes were warriors. The Yanomami tribe made arrowheads out of sharpened monkey bones. They dipped the arrows into a deadly poison called *curare*. These poison arrows were used for hunting and for battles with other tribes.

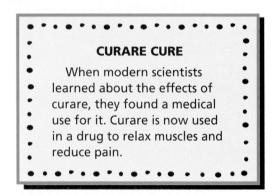

CURARE CURE

When modern scientists learned about the effects of curare, they found a medical use for it. Curare is now used in a drug to relax muscles and reduce pain.

By 1500 A.D., about nine million Indians lived in Brazil. Their lives changed dramatically when explorers arrived from Europe.

THE EUROPEANS ARRIVE

In 1500, a Spanish sailor named Vicente Pinzón landed on the coast of Brazil. He found freshwater flowing into the Atlantic Ocean and traced it back to the Amazon River. Pinzón is now given credit for discovering this important river.

AN INTERESTING CONNECTION TO COLUMBUS

Vicente Pinzón sailed with Christopher Columbus on his first voyage to America. Pinzón was the captain of the Niña. Pinzón's brother was the captain of the Pinta.

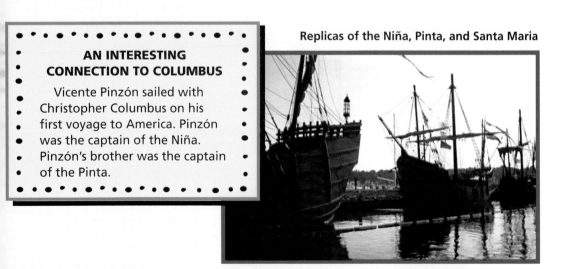

Replicas of the Niña, Pinta, and Santa Maria

That same year, a Portuguese explorer named Pedro Alvares Cabral landed in northeastern Brazil. He was on his way to India to explore the land for the Portuguese king. When Cabral got off course, he ended up in Brazil. Cabral claimed Brazil for Portugal.

By 1530, a group of Portuguese settlers were living in northeastern Brazil. They discovered a tree that produced red and purple dyes. The tree was called *brazilwood*. The Portuguese began shipping the brazilwood dye to Europe. Soon the country became known as "Land of the Brazilwood." Later, the country was simply called Brazil.

As the years passed, more and more settlers arrived in Brazil. One of the largest groups arrived in 1549 when Portugal's king sent 1200 settlers to the **colony**. The settlers' leader, Tome de Sousa, founded Brazil's first capital, Salvador, on the northern coast.

> ## THE TREATY OF TORDESILLAS
>
> Brazil is the only country in South America that was once under Portuguese control. All the other South American countries were claimed and ruled by Spain. This happened because of a document called the Treaty of Tordesillas.
>
> During the 1400s, both Spain and Portugal sent explorers to find a sea route to India and China. These countries had many spices and other valuable items for trading. During these journeys, both Spain and Portugal claimed faraway lands as their own.
>
> To settle arguments over which country had the right to claim these lands, the Pope wrote the Treaty of Tordesillas in 1494. This treaty drew an imaginary line in the western Atlantic. The land that was east of the line was given to Portugal. The land west of the line was given to Spain. Because most of Brazil is east of the Tordesillas line, it became a Portuguese colony.

SLAVERY

The early Portuguese settlers raised sugarcane. To increase their harvest, they captured Indians and forced them to work as slaves. Many of these Indians died from mistreatment. Others died of European diseases, such as smallpox and influenza, brought by the settlers. Because the Indians had never been exposed to these diseases, their bodies could not fight them. By 1700, two-thirds of Brazil's Indians were gone.

In time, the Portuguese needed more slaves to work on their plantations. Since there weren't enough Indians left, they began using slaves from Africa. About three million African slaves were shipped to Brazil from 1600 to 1888. Finally slavery was outlawed in 1888.

EXPLORING THE LAND

At first, European settlers stayed along Brazil's coast. But by the late 1500s, several groups had explored other parts of the country.

Some of these explorers were priests. The priests traveled into the rain forest to **convert** the Indians to Christianity.

During the 1690s, gold and diamonds were discovered in Brazil's interior. Between 1700 and 1800, settlers searching for gold poured into Brazil. The gold mines made Brazil the wealthiest part of the Portuguese empire.

Gold ore

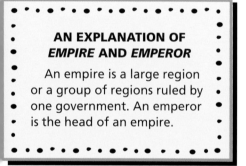

AN EXPLANATION OF EMPIRE AND EMPEROR

An empire is a large region or a group of regions ruled by one government. An emperor is the head of an empire.

During the 18th and 19th centuries, many scientists traveled to Brazil. Two of the most famous were a Frenchman, Charles de La Condamine, and a German, Alexander von Humboldt. These men brought important information about the Amazon Basin and the plants, animals, and people who lived there back to Europe.

Alexander von Humboldt

INDEPENDENCE!

Since 1500, Brazil had been a Portuguese colony. However, many people who lived there wanted to be independent. One of the leaders of the independence movement was a man known as Tiradentes. Tiradentes was inspired by the American and French Revolutions. He dreamed that Brazil could also win its freedom.

Tiradentes and his followers planned to revolt against Portugal. They wanted to rule their own country, make slavery illegal, and help the poor. However, the Portuguese governor found out about the rebels' plans and arrested them. Because he was the leader of the movement, Tiradentes was executed on April 21, 1792. That day is now a national holiday in Brazil.

Although Tiradentes didn't live to see Brazil win its freedom, that day did finally arrive. In 1808, the Portuguese king moved his **court** to Brazil because of a war in Europe. When he finally returned to Portugal in 1821, he left his son, Pedro, in command of Brazil. Pedro felt more loyalty to Brazil than to Portugal because he had grown up in Brazil. So on September 7, 1822, Pedro declared Brazil an independent country. He named himself the country's emperor. From then on, he was known as Dom Pedro I.

Dom Pedro II

FROM EMPIRE TO REPUBLIC

In 1840, Dom Pedro I's son became the emperor. Dom Pedro II ruled for almost 50 years. During his reign, slavery was outlawed. However, the wealthy citizens and the military leaders didn't like Dom Pedro II. He was overthrown in 1889. The new leaders proclaimed that Brazil was a **republic**.

MILITARY RULE

For most of the next 100 years, the military ruled Brazil. Whenever the country had an elected government, the military overthrew it and took control. Between 1889 and 1930, Brazil had 13 different presidents. From 1930 to 1945 and from 1951 to 1954, the country was ruled by a military **dictator**.

Between 1964 and 1984, Brazil was once again under the control of the military. During this time, many people who criticized the government were thrown in jail or killed. There was no freedom of speech or freedom of the press.

A NEW GOVERNMENT

Finally the people of Brazil demanded a new government. In 1989, Brazil elected a president. Since then, the country has been a federal republic. The president is the head of the government. There is also a Federal Senate, a Chamber of Deputies, and a Supreme Court.

Brazil is divided into 26 states and a federal district. Each state and the federal district has its own governor and lawmakers.

COMPARING LEGISLATIVE BRANCHES

The Federal Senate in Brazil is similar to the U.S. Senate, except that each Brazilian state and the federal district has three senators instead of two.

Brazil's Chamber of Deputies is similar to the U.S. House of Representatives. Each Brazilian state has a certain number of elected members in the Chamber based on its population.

CHAPTER 4

Digging In to Brazil's Resources and Industries

RAIN FOREST RESOURCES

The Amazon Rain Forest provides resources for the people of Brazil and the entire world. Trees in the forest are a source of lumber and pulp for paper. Rattan is used to make furniture. String and rope are made from jute. Rubber trees produce latex, a milky liquid used to make rubber.

THE RUNDOWN ON RUBBER

Rubber production is a huge industry in Brazil. Workers called *tappers* collect latex in special cups. Rubber factories employ thousands of Brazilians.

During the 1880s, the demand for rubber soared because cars were becoming popular and rubber was needed to make tires. At that time, the large number of rubber trees in the Amazon made Brazil the world's leading producer of rubber. Many people became rich harvesting this resource. However, by 1914, the rubber boom had come to an end because countries in Southeast Asia began to produce rubber more cheaply. In spite of this, rubber is still an important product in Brazil's **economy**.

Rain forest plants are a bountiful source of foods and spices. Pods from the cacao tree are used to make chocolate. Fruits such as oranges, bananas, pineapples, and coconuts are plentiful. Everyday foods such as coffee, sugar, and vanilla come from the rain forest. Peanuts, cashews, and Brazil nuts are Amazon treats. Thanks to the rain forest, cooks can spice up foods with pepper, ginger, cinnamon, and many other spices.

Many medicines contain ingredients from the rain forest. Alkaloids are substances found in tropical plants. They are used in fever reducers, painkillers, muscle relaxants, and cancer drugs. Quinine comes from the bark of the cinchona tree. This drug is used to fight headaches and infections such as pneumonia. Hundreds of other ingredients for medicines come from the rain forest as well.

WATER

Water is a plentiful resource in most of Brazil. Plants, animals, and people in the country depend on the Amazon River for their water supply. Twenty percent of the world's freshwater flows across Brazil in the Amazon Basin.

In addition, the river water is also used to create electric power. More than 90 percent of Brazil's electricity is produced by hydroelectric plants powered by water.

Dams have been built on many rivers in Brazil to harness hydroelectric power. The largest of these dams is the Tucurui Dam on the eastern edge of the Amazon Basin.

A POWERFUL COUNTRY

The Itaipú power plant on the Brazil-Paraguay border is the largest hydroelectric plant in the world.

MINERALS

Brazil is rich in mineral resources. The country is a leading producer of iron ore. Manganese, copper, zinc, bauxite (used to make aluminum), nickel, and tin are also mined.

Gold was first discovered in Brazil in 1690. It is found in many parts of the Amazon Basin. Over the years, millions of people have searched for gold in the Amazon. Huge machines are used to dig through the mud, sand, and rocks to find the precious metal hidden underneath.

WHAT A GEM!

Gemstones are beautiful, rare rocks or minerals used for decorations. Diamonds, topazes, amethysts, and emeralds are a few gems. Brazil produces 90 percent of the world's gemstones.

AGRICULTURE

Brazil is the world's leading producer of sugar and coffee. Rice, wheat, cotton, and soybeans are common sights in farmers' fields. Citrus fruits, avocados, and grapes grow in the rain forest and in southern Brazil. Oranges and orange juice are a billion-dollar industry in the country.

The southern part of Brazil has fertile land used for large-scale farming and ranching. Huge coffee plantations thrive in the cool climate and rich soil. Beef cattle are also raised in this region of the country.

Coffee plantation

CHAPTER 5

The Many Faces of Brazil

Discovering Brazil's People

IMMIGRANTS AND NATIVES

Brazil's population has its roots in many different countries. More than half of the people who live in Brazil are of European **descent**. Large groups of settlers came to Brazil from Germany, Italy, Spain, and Portugal.

Over time, many Indians and Portuguese settlers married. Africans also married members of other ethnic groups. As a result, Brazilians are a rich blend of several cultures.

> **CULTURE CONNECTION**
>
> Brazil has the largest population of Japanese people other than Japan itself.

The Brazilian Indians who first occupied much of the country now make up only a small part of the population. Most of them live in the Amazon Basin.

Rio de Janeiro

LIFE IN THE CITIES

In the past, most of Brazil's population lived in **rural** areas. However, during recent years, Brazil has become more **urban**. Many people have moved from the country to the city to find jobs and a better way of life.

Brazilian cities look just like big cities in the United States. Cities such as São Paulo and Rio de Janeiro have high-rise buildings and skyscrapers. The streets are crowded with buses and cars. Tall apartment buildings house people living in downtown areas. Others live in modern apartments or houses in the suburbs.

Brazilians work in offices, factories, stores, and restaurants. Others drive taxis, sell flowers, deliver groceries or packages, and clean offices. Poor children often wash cars or shine shoes to make extra money for their families.

Some areas of Brazilian cities are very poor. These places are called *favelas*. The houses in favelas are tiny shacks made of brick or wood. Their roofs are made of **corrugated** iron. The favelas often have no plumbing or electricity.

A favela

WHERE DO THEY LIVE?

Most of Brazil's population lives on or near the coasts. More than half live in big cities. Although the Amazon Basin is large in area, very few people live there.

THE CAPITAL CITY

Brazil's current capital city has an interesting history. Juscelino Kubitschek de Oliveira was president of Brazil from 1955 to 1960. At that time, the coastal city of Rio de Janeiro was the capital of Brazil. Kubitschek wanted to change the capital to a city away from the coast to help develop the inner regions of the country. During his presidency, a new capital city was planned and built. Brasília became the capital of Brazil on April 21, 1960.

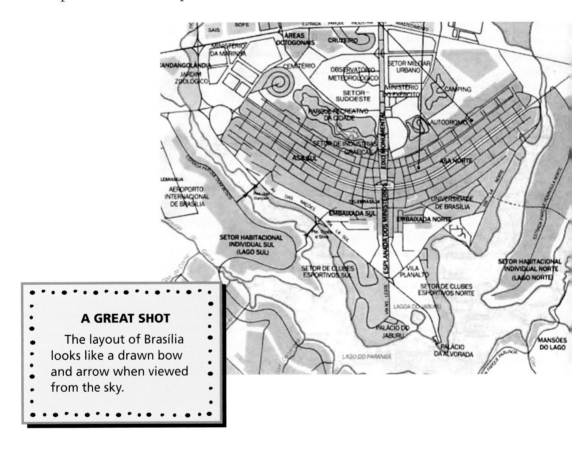

A GREAT SHOT

The layout of Brasília looks like a drawn bow and arrow when viewed from the sky.

LIFE IN THE COUNTRYSIDE

Life in the Brazilian countryside is very different from life in the cities. People who live in rural areas usually work on sugarcane plantations, farms, or ranches. Many families raise cows, pigs, and chickens for food. Other people make baskets or wood items such as furniture. Some rural residents travel to nearby cities for work.

Rural homes are quite different from those in the cities. Many are built of stone or mud bricks. Because the land along the Amazon riverbanks can flood, houses in this area are built on stilts. These houses are usually made of wood or sturdy rain forest plants and have roofs made of palm leaves. Most rural houses have only three or four small rooms. Some have electricity and running water, but many do not.

FAMILY LIFE

Whether they live in the city or country, Brazilians value family life and have many children. In addition to parents and children, Brazilian families have close ties to grandparents, aunts, uncles, and cousins. Hundreds of people might attend an important family event, such as a birthday party or wedding.

CHAPTER 6

A Slice of Life

Brazilian Culture

FOOD

The food of Brazil is as varied as its people. Each region of the country has its own unique flavors and specialties. African foods can be found in the northeastern part of the country. People who live near the Amazon enjoy fish and seafood. Southerners enjoy roasted beef. People all over Brazil eat rice, manioc, and beans. Chicken and duck are also popular.

Because most of Brazil has a tropical climate, many different fruits grow there. Bananas, pineapples, melons, strawberries, papayas, and mangoes are just a few.

Brazil's national dish is *feijoada*. Feijoada is a stew made of pork, black beans, rice, manioc flour, kale, and orange slices.

Coffee is an important part of Brazilian meals. Adults drink a very strong coffee called *cafezinho*. Even children drink coffee in Brazil!

Papaya

BRAZILIAN BRIGADEIROS

Brigadeiros, or chocolate balls, are a delicious candy often served at birthday parties in Brazil. These candies are named after Brigadeiro Eduardo Gomes, an air force pilot who ran for president in Brazil. *Brigadeiro* was his rank in the air force.

ingredients

1 14-ounce can condensed milk

3 tablespoons cocoa powder

1 tablespoon butter

1 cup chocolate sprinkles

directions

1. Mix the condensed milk, butter, and cocoa in a pan.

2. Ask an adult to help you cook the mixture over medium heat. Stirring frequently, cook the mixture until it starts to pull away from the sides of the pan. It should look like a thick paste when it's done.

3. Remove the candy from the heat and let it cool.

4. Grease your hands with a little bit of butter. Roll the candy into small balls.

5. Spread the chocolate sprinkles on a plate or piece of waxed paper.

6. Roll the balls in the sprinkles until they're completely covered.

HOLIDAYS

Religious holidays are especially important in Brazil because most Brazilians are Catholic. Christmas, Easter, and days that honor specific saints are celebrated by most of the country. On these days, Brazilians go to church, eat special foods, and gather with friends and family. They also wear traditional clothing, such as flowered skirts and straw hats. Bonfires sometimes burn all night for saint-day celebrations.

The wildest and most colorful Brazilian holiday is Carnaval. Carnaval is held in February or March during the last few days before the Easter season begins. During Carnaval, the streets are filled with music. People wearing costumes play instruments, sing, and dance. Many participate in parades and attend parties. People come from all over the world to join Brazil's Carnaval celebrations.

Costumes are essential to Brazil's Carnaval. Masks, glitter, and feathers are traditional costume decorations.

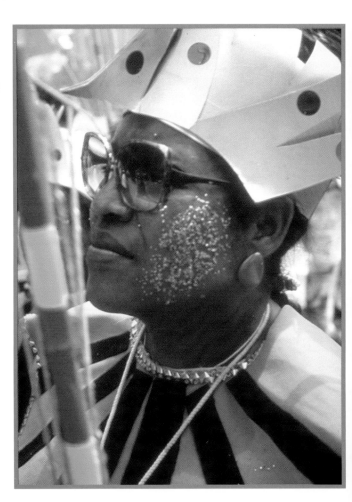

NOTES ON THE NATIONAL HOLIDAYS IN BRAZIL

January 1	New Year's Day
February/March	Carnaval
March/April	Good Friday/Easter Sunday
April 21	Tiradentes Day (honors the execution of Tiradentes in 1792)
May 1	Labor Day
June (60 days after Easter)	Corpus Christi
September 7	Independence Day (anniversary of the declaration of independence from Portugal by Dom Pedro I in 1822)
October 12	Our Lady of Aparecida (patron saint of Brazil)
November 2	All Souls' Day (also called Day of the Dead)
November 15	Proclamation of the Republic Day (anniversary of the day when Dom Pedro II was removed from power in 1889)
December 25	Christmas

Months of preparation are spent on Carnaval parades consisting of elaborate themes, music, costumes, and floats.

EDUCATION

Brazilian law says that all children between the ages of 7 and 14 must go to school. The school year is March to December.

Most students in Brazil wear uniforms. Boys wear dark pants and white shirts. Girls wear dark skirts and white blouses. Both boys and girls wear badges with their school's name on them.

The public schools in Brazil are very crowded. They do not have enough books or supplies for all students. So in some schools, one group of students goes to school in the morning, while another group goes in the afternoon.

Students ages 15 to 18 can attend public or private high schools. But fewer than half of the teenagers in Brazil actually continue their education after age 14. Most leave school to get jobs to earn money for their families. Those who choose to can also go on to colleges or technical schools after high school.

SCHOOL ON TV

In some isolated or poor areas of Brazil, children attend school by listening to programs on TV or the radio.

LANGUAGE

The early Portuguese presence in Brazil resulted in Portuguese becoming the official language of the country. It is spoken in all areas of Brazil, except in the Amazon where the Indians still speak their traditional languages.

SAY "PLEASE" IN PORTUGUESE
Here are a few common expressions and how to say them in Portuguese.

English	Portuguese
please	faz favor (fahz fah VOR)
thank you	obrigado (oh bree GAH doo)
yes	sim (seem)
no	não (now)
good morning	bom dia (bohn GEE yah)
good night	boa noite (bwa NOY chee)
good-bye	adeus (ah DAY oos)

SPORTS

The most popular sport in Brazil is *futebol*, or soccer. Brazil has millions of soccer players and thousands of teams. The best players go on to play in the international soccer championships called the World Cup. Brazil won its fifth World Cup in 2002. That's more World Cups than any other country has won.

PELÉ

Who is the greatest soccer player of all time? Many people think it is a Brazilian named Edson Arantes do Nascimento—better known as Pelé. Pelé started playing professional soccer when he was 15 years old. During the next 18 years, he scored more than 1200 goals and led Brazil to 3 World Cup championships.

Pelé retired from Brazilian soccer in 1974. From 1975 to 1977, he played for the New York Cosmos soccer team in the United States. Later he became part of the Brazilian government, serving as the Minister of Sports.

A HUGE GOAL

Maracanã Stadium in Rio de Janeiro is the largest soccer stadium in the world. It holds 200,000 people.

Auto racing continues to grow in popularity in Brazil. A Brazilian Grand Prix race is held in São Paulo or Rio de Janeiro every year. Ayrton Senna and Emerson Fittipaldi are two of Brazil's most successful auto racers.

Volleyball, basketball, and tennis are professional and recreational sports enjoyed in Brazil. People who live near Brazil's coast swim, boat, and surf in the Atlantic Ocean.

Samba dancer

THE ARTS

Brazil has a rich tradition of art, dancing, and music. Before the Portuguese arrived in the 1500s, the Indians created animal masks, pottery, jewelry, and baskets. Portuguese settlers followed European traditions and styles and brought a different kind of art to Brazil. They often focused on religious subjects for their work.

Later, artists created new styles that featured the bright colors of Brazil's tropical climate. One of the most famous Brazilian artists is Candido Portinari. Some of his paintings hang in the United Nations building in New York City.

Dance is a very expressive part of Brazilian culture. Samba is both a style of music and a type of dance. Samba comes from a combination of traditional Portuguese songs, African rhythms, and Indian dance. It features a lively beat and rhythmic movements.

Capoeira is another Brazilian dance. It is also considered a form of martial arts. Slaves invented capoeira when their masters punished them for fighting. The slaves disguised their fights by making them look like dances. Capoeira dancers use only their legs, feet, and heads. They don't move their hands.

Brazil is also home to a type of music known as bossa nova. *Bossa nova* means "new beat." This type of music combines samba with American jazz rhythms.

CHRIST THE REDEEMER

One of Brazil's best-known pieces of artwork is the statue of Christ the Redeemer. This huge figure is located on Corcovado Mountain, just outside Rio de Janeiro. The statue stands with its arms outstretched to welcome visitors to the city. It stands 100 feet tall and rests on a 22-foot-tall pedestal. Inside the pedestal is a small chapel.

The Christ the Redeemer statue is one of the tallest statues in the world. It was built by sculptor Paul Landowski and engineer Heitor da Silva Costa. It was completed and unveiled in 1931.

What's Ahead?

A Look at Brazil's Future

Brazil is a land of great beauty and riches. But it is also a land of great poverty and hardship. Brazil will need to confront its struggles with a growing population, deforestation, and pollution in order to provide a good quality of life for all of its citizens.

A GROWING POPULATION

Brazil's population is growing very quickly. The country adds about 4.5 million people to its population every year. It is estimated that by the year 2025, Brazil will be home to 250 million people. All of these people need jobs, homes, schools, food, and medical care.

In addition, a large number of Brazilians are already desperately poor. Millions of people have moved from rural areas to the cities hoping to find better-paying jobs. Unfortunately, this has led to an increase in poverty and overcrowding in the cities.

Brazil's natural resources may not be able to support the growing population. The government must plan carefully to spread out the country's wealth among all of its people.

DEFORESTATION

Brazil is home to the largest rain forest in the world. Sadly, that rain forest—and the animals, plants, and people that live in it—is disappearing at a frightening rate. An area of the forest the size of 14 football fields is destroyed every minute.

Deforestation is the removal of many trees from an area. When too many trees are removed, the soil washes away and the land becomes useless for growing. Habitats are destroyed, leaving animals and people homeless.

Deforestation in the Amazon has several causes. Huge areas of land have been cleared for growing crops and grazing cattle. Individuals, companies, and the government have burned or cut down millions of acres of rain forest to clear land for homes, roads, ranches, and farms. Other rain forest trees have been chopped down and used for firewood and building materials or to make paper. Products from rain forest plants are removed carelessly, damaging the forest. All of these causes have resulted in a huge loss of productive rain forest land in Brazil.

In recent years, Brazil's government, **conservation** groups, and many businesses have taken steps to replant trees and set limits and guidelines for removing resources from the rain forest.

POLLUTION

Pollution is also a serious problem in Brazil. The country's large cities are often covered in a brown haze of smog. Sometimes the air quality is so bad that people are warned to stay inside. Rivers have also been polluted by chemicals and waste materials produced by factories, businesses, and homes.

In 1992, Rio de Janeiro was the site of the world's first Earth Summit. Leaders from all over the world met to discuss new laws and other ways to ensure clean air and water for everyone.

LOOKING FORWARD

Brazil faces many changes in the 21st century. However, it has the resources, people, and traditions to make the country a prosperous and enjoyable place to live for all of its citizens.

INTERNET CONNECTIONS AND RELATED READING FOR BRAZIL

Just the Facts!

http://memory.loc.gov/frd/cs/brtoc.html
This Web site is packed with facts on Brazil's history, geography, resources, economy, and government.

http://www.infoplease.com/ipa/A0107357.html
For more quick information and a map of Brazil, visit this site.

http://www.brasilemb.org/kids_corner/kids1.shtml
The Brazilian Embassy in Washington provides a profile of fast facts on Brazil as well as a more detailed description of the country's economy, environment, culture, and tourist attractions.

http://www.timeforkids.com/TFK/specials/goplaces/0,12405,104221,00.html
Time for Kids interviews Brazilian students who share their insights on Brazil and its culture. Go sightseeing, see some Amazon animals, and get an overview of the country's history as well.

Chapter 1

http://www.amazonteam.org/kids/kids6.html
Meet the Mighty Amazon River with this site's facts, figures, and key ideas about this powerful river.

http://www.amazoniafunquest.org/
Go on a quest for knowledge of the Amazon at this fun and educational site.

http://www.livinglakes.org/pantanal/
Find out more about the Pantanal wetlands, including its characteristics, wildlife, and human interactions.

Chapter 2

http://www.srl.caltech.edu/personnel/krubal/rainforest/Edit560s6/www/plants.html
Take time to smell the flowers (and plants) at this "plants of the rainforest" site, which includes epiphytes, bromeliads, lianas, strangler figs, and others.

http://jajhs.kana.k12.wv.us/amazon/animal.htm
Go on an Amazon animal adventure with the pictures and information at this site.

Chapter 3

http://www.timeforkids.com/TFK/specials/goplaces/0,12405,104794,00.html
This timeline of important events in Brazil's history was made for kids.

http://oregon.uoregon.edu/~sergiok/brasilpol.html
Read a brief overview of Brazil's Constitution and three branches of government.

http://www.zoomwhales.com/explorers/1700.shtml
Discover Alexander von Humboldt, Charles de la Condamine, and other important explorers.

Chapter 4

http://www.rainforest-alliance.org/resources/index.html
How much do you depend on the rain forest? This site on rain forest resources will amaze you.

http://www.brazilianconsulate.org.hk/ehtml/about_lon_econ_agriculture.htm
From bananas to coffee beans, find out what's growing in Brazil.

Chapter 5

http://www.brazilianconsulate.org.hk/ehtml/about_was_people.htm
Learn more about Brazil's people and the regions and cities where they live.

http://www.infobrasilia.com.br/bsb_hi.htm
The history of Brazil's capital city, Brasília, is described in detail. The site includes a timeline of the city's history, information on its construction, and biographies of important people.

Chapter 6

http://www.brazilhouston.org/ingles/flavors.htm
Taste the flavors of Brazil with this overview of foods by regions.

http://www.brazilbrazil.com/
Experience Brazilian culture at this colorful, informative Web site packed with facts, figures, and fun.

Chapter 7

http://www.timeforkids.com/TFK/magazines/story/0,6277,90032,00.html
It's time to stop deforestation of the Amazon rain forest! Read this *Time for Kids* article on the disappearance of the Brazilian rain forest and what the country is doing about the problem.

http://darkwing.uoregon.edu/~sergiok/brasil.html
Get up-to-date information on Brazil's current events, news, economy, social issues, and more with the facts and links found at this site.

∘ ∘ ∘ ∘ ∘ ∘ ∘ ∘ ∘ ∘ ∘ ∘ ∘ ∘

Animal Geography: South America by Joanne Mattern. Many unusual animals make their homes in the variety of habitats found in South America. Perfection Learning Corporation, 2002. [RL 4.7 IL 4–9] (3858501 PB 3858502 CC)

Canopies in the Clouds: Earth's Rain Forests by Ellen Hopkins. Take a journey to the Amazon Rain Forest, and learn about the plants and animals that live there. Find out what is being done to save this natural resource. Perfection Learning Corporation, 2002. [RL 4.8 IL 4–9] (3243101 PB 3243102 CC)

Dropping In On Brazil by David C. King. A title in the Dropping In On series. Rourke Book, Co., 1995. [RL 5.5 IL 3–8] (5877306 HB)

• RL = Reading Level
• IL = Interest Level
Perfection Learning's catalog numbers are included for your ordering convenience. PB indicates paperback. CC indicates Cover Craft. HB indicates hardback.

GLOSSARY

basin   (BAY sin) area of land surrounding a river and its tributaries (see separate entry for *tributary*)

colony   (KAHL uh nee) settlement in one land ruled by another country

conservation   (kon ser VAY shun) protection of natural resources

convert   (kuhn VERT) to change from one belief to another

corrugated   (KOR uh gay ted) wrinkled or folded

court   (kort) king or queen's group of advisors and officers

descent   (di SENT) coming from a particular place; heritage

dictator   (DIK tay ter) person with complete control over a country

economy   (ee KON uh mee) country's system of making, buying, and selling goods and services

federal republic   (FED er uhl ree PUHB lik) country with a strong central government elected by the citizens

fertile   (FER tuhl) good for growing

fungus   (FUHNG uhs) organisms that can't produce their own food (see separate entry for *organism*)

native   (NAY tiv) originally living in an area

organism   (OR guh niz uhm) living thing

plateau   (plat OH) large raised area of land with a flat surface

predator   (PRED uh ter) animal that hunts other animals for food

prey   (pray) animal that is hunted by other animals for food

epublic   (ree PUHB lik) government with an elected head, usually a president

odent   (ROH dent) gnawing animal

ural   (ROOR uhl) having to do with life in the country

hrub   (shruhb) plant or bush that is low to the ground

emperate   (TEMP ruht) having temperatures that are neither too hot nor too cold; mild

ributary   (TRIB you tair ee) smaller body of water that flows into a river

urban   (ER bin) having to do with life in the city

Street markets, also known as *feiras*, are common in Brazil. Vendors sell clothing, crafts, fruits, vegetables, fish, and other items. This fiera is in Recife, Brazil.

INDEX

agriculture, 26
Amazon Basin, 7–8, 10, 26
Amazon Rain Forest, 7, 8, 24–25
Amazon River, 7, 8, 19
animals, 13–17
    Amazon River dolphin, 14
    capybara, 14
    green iguana, 16
    jaguar, 13
    leaf-cutting ant, 17
    macaw, 15
    pampas cat, 17
    pampas deer, 17
    parrot, 15
    piranha, 15
    poison dart frog, 16–17
    tapir, 13
    three-toed sloth, 14
    toucan, 15
    vampire bat, 14
area, 4, 7
arts, 39–40
    bossa nova, 40
    capoeira, 40
    Portinari, Candido, 39
    samba, 39
Cabral, Pedro Alvares, 20
capital city, 5, 30
Christ the Redeemer statue, 40

cities
    Brasília, 5, 30
    Rio de Janiero, 5
    Salvador, 5
    São Paulo, 5
climate, 5, 10
currency, 6
deforestation, 42
Dom Pedro I, 22
Dom Pedro II, 22
education, 36
elevation, 4
favelas, 29
Fittipaldi, Emerson, 39
flag, 6
foods, 32–33
government, 5, 23
Great Escarpment, 9
holidays, 34–35
    Carnaval, 34, 35
homes, 28, 29, 31
Humboldt, Alexander von, 21
Iguacu River, 9
Indians, 18–19
    Yanomami, 19
industries, 6
La Condamine, Charles de, 21
language, 5, 37
location, 4
minerals, 6, 26

natural resources, 6
Oliveira, Juscelino Kubitschek de, 30
pampas, 9, 12, 17
Pantanal, 9
Pelé, 38
Pinzón, Vicente, 19
plants, 11–12
    climbing, 12
    epiphytes, 12
pollution, 43
population, 5, 41
products of the rain forest, 12, 19,
    24–25
    curare, 19
    foods, 25
    medicines, 12, 25
    rubber, 24
religion, 5, 34
Senna, Ayrton, 39
sertão, 9, 10, 12
slavery, 20–21
Sousa, Tome de, 20
sports, 37–39
states, 6
Tiradentes (Joaquim José de Silva
    Xavier), 22
Treaty of Tordesillas, 20
water, 25
    Itaipú power plant, 25
    Tucurui Dam, 25